# DIWALI
## A First Look

### PERCY LEED

GRL Consultant, Diane Craig, Certified Literacy Specialist
Content Consultant, Deven Patel, Professor of South Asia Studies, University of Pennsylvania

Lerner Publications ◆ Minneapolis

# TABLE OF CONTENTS

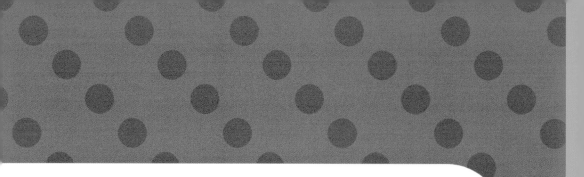

## Diwali

**Diwali is a holiday in India.**

It is also called the
Festival of Lights.

People light small
oil lamps.

They put them outside.

Diwali lasts five days.
People get ready the
first two days.
They make their
homes pretty.

The third day
is the biggest.
Families dress up.
They pray.

When does your family dress up?

Fireworks light
the sky.

Families have
big meals.
They also
eat sweets.

When else do people
have big meals?

There are two more days. People visit family and friends. They give gifts.

When do you
give gifts?

Diwali is India's biggest holiday.
It is a happy time.

## You Connect!

Do you celebrate Diwali?

When do you gather with family?

What is something you have done or would like to do for Diwali?

# Social and Emotional Snapshot

Student voice is crucial to building reader confidence. Ask the reader:

What is your favorite part of this book?

What is something you learned from this book?

Did this book remind you of any other holidays you celebrate?

Opportunities for social and emotional learning are everywhere. How can you connect the topic of this book to the SEL competencies below?

Self-Awareness
Relationship Skills
Social Awareness

# Photo Glossary

fireworks

lights

oil lamps

pray

# Learn More

Leed, Percy. *Lunar New Year: A First Look*. Minneapolis: Lerner Publications, 2023.

Schuh, Mari. *Crayola Diwali Colors*. Minneapolis: Lerner Publications, 2019.

Umrigar, Thrity. *Binny's Diwali*. New York: Scholastic Press, 2020.

# Index

## Photo Acknowledgments

The images in this book are used with the permission of: © StockImageFactory.com/Shutterstock Images, pp. 4–5; © Deepak Sethi/iStockphoto, pp. 6–7; © Navoditaa/iStockphoto, pp. 7, 23 (top right); © Toa55/iStockphoto, pp. 8, 23 (bottom left); © SOMNATH CHATTERJEE/iStockphoto, p. 9; © PRASANNAPIX/Shutterstock Images, pp. 10–11; © FatCamera/iStockphoto, pp. 12, 23 (bottom right); © szefei/iStockphoto, pp. 12–13; © Abhishek Vyas/iStockphoto, pp. 14–15, 23 (top left); © Rangeecha/iStockphoto, pp. 16–17; © subodhsathe/iStockphoto, pp. 18–19; © triloks/iStockphoto, p. 20.

Cover Photo: © NIDHI/iStockphoto.

Design Elements: © Mighty Media, Inc.

Lerner Publications Company
An imprint of Lerner Publishing Group, Inc.
241 First Avenue North
Minneapolis, MN 55401 USA

For reading levels and more information, look up this title at www.lernerbooks.com.

Main body text set in Mikado a Medium.
Typeface provided by Hannes von Doehren.

**Library of Congress Cataloging-in-Publication Data**

Names: Leed, Percy, 1968–. author.
Title: Diwali : a first look / Percy Leed.
Description: Minneapolis : Lerner Publications, 2023. | Series: Read about holidays. Read for a better world | Includes bibliographical references and index. | Audience: Ages 5–8 | Audience: Grades K–1 | Summary: "Diwali is an Indian holiday known as the Festival of Lights. Simple text and full-color photos give young learners a look at this happy holiday"– Provided by publisher.
Identifiers: LCCN 2022010029 (print) | LCCN 2022010030 (ebook) | ISBN 9781728475622 (library binding) | ISBN 9781728478951 (paperback) | ISBN 9781728484105 (ebook)
Subjects: LCSH: Divali–Juvenile literature. | India–Social life and customs–Juvenile literature.
Classification: LCC BL1239.82.D58 L44 2023 (print) | LCC BL1239.82.D58 (ebook) | DDC 394.265/45–dc23/eng/20220413

LC record available at https://lccn.loc.gov/2022010029
LC ebook record available at https://lccn.loc.gov/2022010030

Manufactured in the United States of America
2-1009340-50592-3/17/2023